CW01498189

Original title:

Fallow Sprigs Under the Dragon Yew

Author: Swan Charm

ISBN HARDBACK: 978-1-80562-858-3

ISBN PAPERBACK: 978-1-80564-379-1

Roots that Kiss the Darkness

Deep below the ancient oak,
Whispers of the night invoke.
Branches sway with secrets old,
Where stories of the dark unfold.

Murmurs in the restless ground,
Echoes of the lost, profound.
With every sigh, the shadows creep,
And through the roots, the spirits seep.

Beneath the soil, life intertwines,
Glimmers of fate in twisted vines.
A dance of shadows, soft and stark,
In quiet corners where dreams embark.

A realm where light dares not to roam,
The heart of darkness finds its home.
In tangled masses, spirits scheme,
To hold the light, to weave a dream.

Yet from the gloom, a spark may rise,
An ember flickers, illuminating skies.
Roots that kiss the dark embrace,
Bring forth the light to this hidden place.

Tales Woven in Twilight Shadows

As dusk descends with gentle grace,
The stars prepare to haunt their space.
Whispers float on the evening breeze,
Tales untold in the twilight trees.

Fog drapes softly on the ground,
A silver hush that's all around.
In the stillness, shadows blend,
And secret stories start to mend.

With every rustle, mysteries sway,
Tales of yore that yearn to play.
Fortunes lost, and dreams once bright,
Drawn forth in shades by fading light.

Luminous night, a canvas wide,
Holds the echoes of those who've died.
Their laughter dances through the air,
In twilight shadows, stories share.

So listen close and breathe it in,
The magic where the tales begin.
In every heart, the night will dwell,
Our whispered truths, a timeless spell.

The Matured Serenade of the Forest

Among the trees, where whispers blend,
A melody that has no end.
Leaves sway softly in the breeze,
Nature's song, a sweet reprise.

Time has grown the branches wide,
In their arms, the secrets bide.
With roots that drink from earth's deep well,
A serenade the woods will tell.

Birds of lace and furred grace roam,
Find solace here, their ancient home.
Each note a story of their kin,
In the forest's heart, the song begins.

Golden rays weave through the leaves,
A tapestry that nature weaves.
With every breath, the forest sings,
A harmony of life that brings.

From tiny sprout to towering height,
In union, darkness meets the light.
The matured serenade will play,
In whispered tones, both night and day.

As Time Bows to the Elder Trees

In shadows deep where whispers dwell,
The elder trees weave tales to tell.
With branches high and roots so wide,
They guard the secrets time can't hide.

Upon their bark, the stories lie,
Of lovers lost and dreams that sigh.
Their leaves will dance in autumn's breeze,
As time bows down to elder trees.

The Unfurling of Forgotten Hope

In twilight's glow where wishes fade,
A bud emerges from the shade.
With gentle thoughts and tender light,
It stretches forth to greet the night.

Each petal soft, a promise made,
Of dreams reborn, of fears allayed.
With every blossom's vibrant hue,
Forgotten hope finds life anew.

Tales Beneath the Arboreal Giants

Beneath the boughs where shadows play,
Old giants stand and watch the day.
They whisper truths in rustling leaves,
Of hearts entwined and webs they weave.

The stories run like streams of gold,
Of magic lost and love retold.
In every ring a tale does spin,
Of where the past and present begin.

Glimmers of Life Amidst the Stillness

In quiet woods where silence reigns,
A flicker stirs, a pulse remains.
With every breath, the stillness breaks,
As hidden life awakens, shakes.

The softest glow of fireflies bright,
Dances like whispers in the night.
Amidst the calm, a heartbeat finds,
The glimmers of life the stillness binds.

Beyond the Veil of Greenery

In the hush where shadows creep,
Whispers of the forest keep.
Beneath the boughs, secrets twine,
Lost in dreams, where sunbeams shine.

Mossy carpets softly lay,
Guiding footsteps on their way.
Ferns like fans, in elegance,
Invite you to a hidden dance.

Time cascades in emerald hues,
Where the laughter of the muse
Sings through leaves that shimmer bright,
Awakening the heart's delight.

Wand'ring souls in twilight bound,
Find the magic all around.
In this realm, where stories weave,
Beyond the veil, we dare believe.

Nature's breath, so pure and sweet,
Lingers here where spirits meet.
In every sigh, the thrum of grace,
Unfolds in this enchanted place.

The Patina of Nature's Grace

Upon the bark, a tapestry,
Stories writ in rust and tree.
Each layer tells of time's embrace,
Nature's art, a soft, warm trace.

Golden leaves in autumn's glow,
Whisper secrets on the flow.
Time stands still, yet moves so fast,
Crafting memories long to last.

Crimson berries, jewel-like bright,
Nestle in the fading light.
A gentle sigh, the breeze's song,
Where the heart's wild dreams belong.

Pebbles worn by years gone by,
Echo tales of earth and sky.
In every crack, a life has grown,
In silent paths, the kindness shown.

Nature wraps the world in grace,
Patina shines on every face.
In this realm where we must roam,
Every step leads us back home.

Hopeless Growth in Sunless Nooks

In the corners, shadows cling,
Fragile hopes make soft hearts sing.
Tiny blooms in darkness fight,
Claiming space from sheer delight.

Gnarled roots in silence yearn,
For the light, they twist and turn.
Whispers wane, but life endures,
Finding cracks to seek the pure.

Fungi sprout in shades of grey,
A subtle dance in disarray.
Spirits woven in the dark,
Feed the soil, ignite the spark.

Courage dwells in hidden places,
Where despair leaves tender traces.
Though the sun may hide its cheer,
Life still flourishes year by year.

In shadows deep, the soul can breathe,
Every struggle sows belief.
Hopeful growth, though frail and slight,
Defies the dark, embraces light.

The Language of Abandoned Spaces

In silence, voices softly speak,
Echoes of the past, unique.
Rusting gates and crumbling walls,
Whisper secrets, time enthralls.

A child's laughter, lost in air,
Lingering, like a fading prayer.
Once vibrant hearts now drift away,
Leaving only shadows to stay.

Swaying grass through broken panes,
Nature's touch where stillness reigns.
Every corner, a tale untold,
Of moments cherished, dreams grown old.

Cobwebs weave their gentle lace,
In the stillness, trace their grace.
Forgotten paths that once were bright,
Now bask in the hush of night.

Yet hope persists in every crack,
With every step, a way back.
In abandoned spaces, we find
The language of the heart, aligned.

A Canvas of Nature's Solitude

In the hush of the dawn's first light,
Silence paints the world so bright.
Each shadow whispers, soft and clear,
A symphony that all can hear.

Mist weaves tales through ancient trees,
Dancing gently with the breeze.
A canvas brushed with hues of gold,
Nature's secrets yet untold.

Rivers sing a tranquil song,
Where the heart of Earth belongs.
Pebbles shimmer in the stream,
Reflecting every silent dream.

Buds awaken, stretching wide,
In this sacred, secret ride.
Flocks of birds soar, bold and free,
Sketching arcs of jubilee.

Here, among the tranquil sighs,
Time dissolves and softly flies.
In solitude, the soul takes flight,
In nature's arms, pure, warm delight.

The Elegy of the Lost Seasons

Whispers of autumn weave their spell,
As leaves recount their stories well.
With every rustle, a tale unfolds,
In the air, the past gently holds.

Winter's breath, crisp and cold,
Wraps the world in silver told.
Silent nights with stars that gleam,
Fractured dreams in moonlight stream.

Spring dances in a fragrant bloom,
Filling hearts that once felt gloom.
Life awakens in vibrant hues,
Each petal sings of shared muse.

Yet summer's warmth begins to fade,
Memories linger, softly laid.
The heartbeat of seasons thrum,
In nature's chorus, all is one.

In every season, love and loss,
Echo softly, yet they cross.
The elegy of time unfolds,
In nature's arms, the soul consoles.

Beneath the Twisted Trunks

Beneath the trunks, so gnarled and wise,
The tales of old begin to rise.
Whispers echo through the bark,
In the stillness, a hidden spark.

Roots entwined, in silence stand,
Guardians of this ancient land.
With every knot, a story spun,
Of battles fought and kindness won.

Moss carpets soft the forest floor,
Inviting wanderers to explore.
In shadows deep, the light will play,
From dawn 'til dusk, through night to day.

The twisted trees, a refuge sought,
In their embrace, the world is caught.
Time unwinds beneath their shade,
In this cocoon, all fears betrayed.

Beneath their branches, hearts renew,
Finding peace in nature's view.
In twisted trunks, we find our way,
Where dreams and whispers softly sway.

When Leaves Turn to Memory

When leaves start turning shades of gold,
Memories whisper, tales unfold.
Each flutter dances in the breeze,
Stories carried upon the trees.

Sunset hues ignite the sky,
As daylight bids the world goodbye.
Fragments of laughter intertwine,
In the fading light, hearts align.

Crisp air carries scents of yore,
Beneath the boughs, we yearn for more.
Every crunch beneath our feet,
Echoes of moments bittersweet.

As twilight wraps the day in mist,
We linger on what can't be kissed.
In the silence, love transcends,
When all that's lost, the heart defends.

In memory's arms, we find our place,
And navigate through time and space.
When leaves turn gold, we hold them dear,
For every parting brings us near.

Beneath the Canopy of Time

In shadows deep, the whispers tread,
Though ages pass, the heart is fed.
Each leaf a tale, each branch a dream,
Beneath the boughs, the world may gleam.

The sunbeams dance in golden hues,
Where secrets lie beneath the dews.
A tapestry of twilight skies,
Where fleeting moments softly rise.

The roots entwined, a timeworn thread,
Of stories spun, though long since shed.
Yet in the stillness, magic wakes,
As every sigh the forest makes.

With every step upon the ground,
The echo of the past resounds.
In every rustle, in every sigh,
A melody of by-and-by.

In twilight's glow, the branches sway,
And beckon forth the end of day.
Beneath the canopy, dreams align,
In corners where the stars can shine.

In the Quiet of Verdant Memories

In whispers soft, the meadow sighs,
Where laughter lingers, time complies.
A quilt of green, where shadows play,
In gentle folds, the memories lay.

With petals bright, the blossoms bloom,
Each color paints away the gloom.
In every corner, echoes dwell,
Of stories weave, like magic spell.

A brook that giggles as it flows,
Through meadows lush, where nothing slows.
Each twist and turn, a breath of lore,
In quiet channels, life restores.

As twilight falls, the crickets sing,
The night unfolds with tender wing.
In starlit skies, the dreams arise,
To guide the heart where the past lies.

In silent hours, beneath the trees,
The world transforms with every breeze.
In verdant dreams, we lay our heads,
And drift beyond where silence spreads.

Tendrils of Hope in Enchanted Silence

In silent woods, where magic grows,
The tendrils reach where daylight glows.
Each moment whispers, secrets shared,
In shadows deep, the heart is bared.

The air is thick with ancient tales,
Of heroes bold and ghostly gales.
In every echo, a spark ignites,
To light the way for starry nights.

Among the ferns, the dreams take flight,
With every heartbeat, deep in night.
The stillness hums with hope anew,
In twinkling stars, a window's view.

The branches sway in soft embrace,
Each tendril searching for a trace.
A dance of shadows, beckoning near,
The promise breathed in whispered cheer.

In twilight's grasp, the past may fade,
Yet hope within the silence laid.
For in the dark, the light will steer,
The heart towards all it holds dear.

Glimmers of Life Among Stony Roots

Beneath the stones, where shadows creep,
The roots entwine in silence deep.
Each crack a haven, each crevice holds,
The sighs of life, the tales of old.

Amidst the grit, the wildflowers bloom,
With colors bold dispelling gloom.
They rise against the time's cruel hand,
In defiance strong upon the land.

A whispered breeze through branches plays,
And stirs the whispers of long days.
In every rustle, every breath,
There's life anew, defying death.

The stones may weigh and darken skies,
Yet light will find, in sweet reprise.
For every struggle, every fight,
Brings forth the glimmers of the light.

With every heartbeat, new life starts,
The roots a map of secret parts.
In harmony, they weave and twine,
Among the stones, the stars align.

The Untold Saga of Twisted Vines

In the forest deep, where shadows coil,
Twisted vines whisper, their secrets toil.
Beneath the canopy, stories unwind,
Of ancient spirits the wise have maligned.

Through tangled paths where moonlight weaves,
The heart of nature, in silence, grieves.
Roots like fingers grasp at the past,
Holding tales of a love that couldn't last.

Each leaf a message, each thorn a tear,
A tapestry spun from both joy and fear.
The wind carries fragments of laughter lost,
Echoes of lives that the forest embossed.

As time slips by, they twist and they twine,
Binding memories beneath the pine.
A saga of sorrow, a hymn of delight,
In the heart of the woods, concealed from sight.

So venture forth where the wild things grow,
And listen closely, for they surely know.
The untold saga that nature designs,
Lies hidden within the twisted vines.

Secrets Etched in Old Bark

On the gnarled oak, where wisdom resides,
Secrets are whispered by the woods' old guides.
Etched in the bark, the tales of yore,
Stories of battles, love, and more.

Rain-soaked memories held tight in grain,
Each ring a year, each scar a pain.
With every season, they dance and sway,
Guardians of time, come what may.

The insects scrawl, in delicate script,
Legends of nature, in silence, equipped.
From the roots that delve in the earth so deep,
To the branches reaching where the skylarks leap.

Generations gather, beneath its shade,
While heartbeats echo the paths they've laid.
Secrets nestled in the emerald cloak,
Binding the young to the old oak folk.

So read the bark and let your heart see,
The whispers of ages, wild and free.
For in every crease, a journey waits,
In the ancient tree, where time captivates.

The Resilience of the Undergrowth

In the shadowed glen where silence wakes,
The undergrowth thrives, no matter what breaks.
Through thorns and brambles, they steadfastly cling,
Resilience wrapped in the breath of spring.

Each tiny leaf a soldier, bold,
Defying the chill, the biting cold.
They weave a tapestry, humble and true,
In the heart of the forest, they gently grew.

Sunlight dapples through the canopy high,
A promise of warmth as the seasons sigh.
With roots intertwining, they hold each other,
In the dance of life, each one's a brother.

Amidst the giants that tower so grand,
The undergrowth knows how to withstand.
For hidden below where the wild things play,
Lies strength that endures come what may.

So let us learn from the green and small,
To rise up strong, to answer the call.
In the resilience found within nature's wraith,
Lies a courage untouched by fate.

Hibernation of the Unnoticed

In the quiet hush of a winter's night,
Creatures retreat from the cold and the blight.
Beneath the frost, in holes they dwell,
The unnoticed sleep where dreams softly swell.

With each passing snowflake, a story is spun,
Of lives intertwined beneath the sun.
In burrows they huddle, embraced by the earth,
Waiting for spring to once more give birth.

Silent are the woods, wrapped in white,
Holding secrets close, away from the light.
In the heart of the chill, a warmth resides,
As life prepares for the turning tides.

The rhythm of nature, in stillness profound,
Bears the weight of the dreams underground.
So close your eyes, and listen with care,
To the whispers of life in the chill, so rare.

For in the hibernation, the magic does lie,
The unnoticed thrive as the stars drift by.
And when the dawn calls, and the thaw begins,
Life will awaken, and the dance recommence.

The Forgotten Chronicles of Growth

In shadows deep where whispers weave,
Old tales of growth begin to breathe.
The roots dig down, the branches sway,
Nature's path leads hearts astray.

Through winding paths, the travelers roam,
Each step a quest, yet far from home.
With every sprout, a secret sown,
In forgotten fields, lost dreams are grown.

The seasons shift, a constant thread,
In silent woods where stories tread.
The sunlit glens hold tender grace,
In every corner, time's embrace.

As night descends with silken sighs,
Stars awaken in velvet skies.
They guide the lost, the weary souls,
To realms where growth and wonder pulls.

So heed the tales of bark and stone,
Of whispered dreams, both past and known.
For in the echoes of the earth,
Lies the promise of rebirth.

Beneath the Canopy of Dreams

Beneath the leaves where shadows play,
In realms where light and magic sway,
Dreams take form in vibrant hues,
A tapestry of wondrous views.

Each gentle breeze a secret's song,
Inviting all to sing along.
The whispers float on wings of night,
Guiding hearts to take their flight.

In twilight's glow, the stars align,
Their shimmering dance, a celestial sign.
Visions weave like threads of gold,
In the heart, the stories unfold.

When morning breaks with painted skies,
The world awakes, and hope complies.
Beneath the canopy, life ignites,
With each new dawn, the spirit flights.

So gather dreams like precious gems,
In the forest's arms, the journey stems.
For in the quiet, rich and deep,
Lie the seeds of what we keep.

Resilience in the Forgotten Growth

In silent woods where shadows dwell,
Resilience blooms, a whispered spell.
Through tangled thorns and winding trails,
Defiance grows where courage prevails.

Amidst the storms that test and break,
The roots grip tight, for hope's own sake.
With every fall, the rise is near,
Strength emerges from depths of fear.

The sun may hide, the rain may pour,
Yet each green sprout yearns for more.
In all that bends, in all that's frail,
The heart of growth shall never fail.

As seasons dazzle, shift, and swirl,
In every bud, a dream unfurl.
With every breath, life's pulse is felt,
In every struggle, wisdom's melt.

So nurture strength, let spirits soar,
For every scar, a tale of war.
In forgotten growth, a truth we've known:
The seeds of courage thrive alone.

A Mirror of Nature's Complex Symphony

In every leaf, the music swells,
A symphony where nature dwells.
With rustling notes, the breezes play,
In harmony, they gently sway.

The rivers hum a liquid tune,
Beneath the sun, beneath the moon.
Each creature's call, a part of song,
In nature's choir, we all belong.

As petals dance in sunlit rays,
Life finds rhythm, in myriad ways.
The winds compose, the storms respond,
In this grand play, we are all fond.

From mountain peaks to ocean's song,
The cadence echoes, fierce and strong.
With every heartbeat, life is thread,
A mirror held, where souls are led.

So listen close, in silence deep,
For nature's song is ours to keep.
In every chorus, every tune,
We find our place beneath the moon.

Shadows Entwined with Light

In twilight's embrace, shadows dance bright,
Their tendrils entwined with soft beams of white.
A flicker of hope in the depths of the dark,
Where whispers of dreams leave their shimmering mark.

The moon casts a glow on the secrets we keep,
While starlight weaves tales that shimmer and leap.
In the heart of the night, where fears lose their might,
Together we wander, in shadows, in light.

Memories of a Verdant Realm

In the heart of the forest, where whispers are gold,
Every leaf tells a story of adventures bold.
The streams sing of laughter, the flowers of grace,
In this verdant realm, time has no place.

Beneath canopies woven with soft, dappled shade,
The echoes of childhood in echoes have played.
As light filters down, through branches so wide,
Memories blossom, in nature we bide.

Rebirth Amongst the Ruins

Amidst ancient stones, where the echoes reside,
Resilience awakens, in cracks, it will bide.
Life's tender fingers entwine with decay,
And breathe in the ruins, where hope finds its way.

The past lays its head on the shoulders of time,
While new blooms emerge, in their soft, gentle climb.
Once covered in silence, now sings a sweet tune,
In this dance of rebirth, beneath the bright moon.

Whispers of the Molten Stone

Deep in the earth where the secrets reside,
The molten stone whispers of worlds that have tried.
Eruptions of dreams in a fiery swirl,
A canvas of fate in a tempest unfurl.

In chambers of darkness, where shadows do wane,
Heat bears the stories of love, loss, and gain.
Each crack in the surface reveals tales untold,
And stirs the heart's courage, through warmth, unfolds.

Remnants of Green in Gloomy Realms

In shadowed nooks where sunlight fades,
The whispers weave through emerald glades.
A mossy cloak on ancient stone,
The tales of light in whispers grown.

Through tangled brush, a spark of hue,
A flicker bright, a promise true.
As shadows stretch and daylight dims,
Life clings on, in vibrant whims.

Each leaf a story, each petal a sigh,
Echoes dance beneath the sky.
In gloomy realms where hope once fought,
Remnants of green, a solace sought.

The past unfolds with every breeze,
Memories wrapped in twilight's freeze.
For even dark can't snuff the spark,
Of nature's dream, a secret arc.

Spirits of the Silent Forest

Whispers drift through towering pines,
Where shadows weave and mystery shines.
Beneath the boughs, old secrets dwell,
In silence deep, they cast their spell.

A flicker here, a shuffled leaf,
The forest breathes, a sigh, a creak.
With every step, the spirits sway,
In rhythmic dance, they find their play.

Moonbeams cast a silver thread,
To guide the lost, to those long dead.
In twilight's grace, they spin and weave,
A tranquil depth, in hearts they cleave.

Their murmurs float on evening's air,
A gentle balm, a loving care.
For every soul that wanders near,
In silent woods, they'll find their cheer.

The Dance of Shadows and Light

With twilight's hand, the shadows rise,
As stars awaken in velvet skies.
A waltz begins on the forest floor,
Where light and dark forever implore.

They twirl in circles, a perfect spin,
A harmony found where dreams begin.
Each flicker bold, each silhouette,
A dance of fate, a soft duet.

The world, it glistens, a whispering sigh,
As colors bloom and shadows fly.
In every flick, a tale unfolds,
In the night's embrace, new dreams are sold.

So let them dance 'til morning's break,
A fleeting pause in the journey's wake.
For even shadows, with hearts so bright,
Are part of the magic, a pure delight.

Echoes of the Earthbound Dreamers

Beneath the stars, the dreamers tread,
With whispered hopes and stories spread.
In gentle murmurs, they softly weave,
A tapestry of all they believe.

With every heartbeat, the earth can feel,
The echoes rise; they start to heal.
Each sigh and laugh, a tethered thought,
In the dance of dreams, they boldly sought.

They plant their wishes in the soil,
Through storms and sun, in patient toil.
For every dawn that breaks anew,
The earthbound souls revive their view.

So listen close, and you might hear,
The songs of dreamers, both far and near.
In every rustle, in every breeze,
Are whispers of lives that aim to please.

Amongst the Twisting Vines of Fate

In the garden where shadows play,
The vines curl and twist in dismay.
Each leaf a tale of love and woe,
Beneath the moon's soft, silver glow.

Whispers weave through the silent air,
Fates entwined in the mystic glare.
Time's embrace, both cruel and kind,
In every stalk, a secret bind.

With lanterns lit by stars above,
Hearts discover the strength of love.
Through thorns we tread, we find our way,
As tangled roots of dreams hold sway.

Life's dance unfolds, a waltz so sweet,
Where destiny and courage meet.
Amidst the chaos, hope ignites,
In every twist, our heart takes flight.

So linger here, beneath the sky,
Where twisted vines and dreams comply.
For in this maze, we're not alone,
In every path, our spirits grown.

Where the Wild Things Whisper

In lands where wild things softly tread,
Each whisper dances, words unsaid.
Mossy paths where spirits roam,
In crickets' songs, we find our home.

Beneath the boughs of ancient trees,
The secrets ride upon the breeze.
Tales of heroes, lost and found,
In every rustle, magic's sound.

Moonlight bathes the forgotten trails,
Where laughter echoes, hope prevails.
Beneath the stars, we twirl and sway,
Where wild things come to seize the day.

With every step, the heartbeats sync,
In this wild realm, we pause and think.
What stories in the shadows hide,
Where dreams collide, and hearts abide?

So venture forth, let spirits soar,
Where wild things whisper—fear no more.
In every breath, adventure calls,
Through wooded halls, the wonder sprawls.

Serenity in the Depths of Green

In emerald woods where silence rests,
A sanctuary, nature's best.
Soft light filters through the leaves,
Where tranquility gently weaves.

Streams babble secrets, clear and bright,
In soothing whispers, day turns night.
With every rustle, dreams awake,
In the heart of green, the soul can break.

Beneath the canopy, we breathe deep,
In emerald spaces where shadows creep.
Time slows down, the chaos fades,
In this refuge, our hearts cascade.

Here in stillness, fears dissolve,
Within the green, our worlds evolve.
Nature cradles our worries near,
In depths of green, joy reappears.

So come and rest amidst the trees,
Embrace the calm, the gentle breeze.
In serenity, our spirits gleam,
In the depths of green, life's sweet dream.

Roots Reaching for Forgotten Stars

Beneath the soil, deep and dark,
Roots stretch forth with a hopeful spark.
Seeking light on paths unseen,
To touch the stars and chase the sheen.

In layers thick where shadows dwell,
Every whisper tells a tale to tell.
Of ancient dreams both lost and found,
And echoes in the underground.

Branches lift towards the cosmic sea,
In yearning arcs, they long to be.
Embracing light, as dawn breaks wide,
With roots that fight the rising tide.

In the stillness, hearts align,
For growth begins where stars combine.
Through soil and stone, a journey starts,
Roots reaching forth for forgotten arts.

So linger here beneath the night,
Where roots reach deep for that lost light.
In every struggle, every scar,
We find our place amongst the stars.

Whispers Beneath the Ancient Canopy

Beneath the boughs of emerald dreams,
Soft murmurs weave through golden beams.
In twilight's hush, secrets unfold,
Tales of magic, from days of old.

Leaves rustle gently, stories in flight,
Echoes of laughter, a flicker of light.
The canopy holds, what time won't betray,
The whispers of souls, who danced in the day.

Shadows waltz with the light's embrace,
Nature's grace painted on every face.
The wind sings softly, a ballad so fair,
As dreams intertwine with the cool, evening air.

Moonlight spills like silver lore,
Each branching tale leads to the forest floor.
With every sigh, the night deepens still,
Longing to hear what the heart may fulfill.

A sentinel stands, with roots intertwined,
Guarding the dreams that the ancients enshrined.
In the heart of the grove, where magic runs free,
The whispers call out, inviting you near.

Shadows of the Forgotten Grove

In the grove where the shadows play,
Memories linger, lost in the gray.
Once vibrant blooms now fade from sight,
Silhouettes dance in the hush of night.

The trees wear crowns of tangled vines,
Holding the dreams of forgotten signs.
Whispers of laughter, now distant and rare,
Echo through twilight, heavy with care.

Footsteps muffled on the soft, damp earth,
Recounting tales of both sorrow and mirth.
Ghostly figures brush past the pines,
Characters lost, caught in the vines.

With every gust, the branches sigh,
Relics of magic beneath the sky.
The moon casts shadows, deep and profound,
In the embrace of night, where dreams are unbound.

In this haven so wild and untamed,
Unearthed whispers of love unclaimed.
The grove awaits with each fading light,
As echoes of history blend with the night.

Lament of the Withered Branches

Oh, withered branches, once proud and strong,
Your melodies fade, like a forgotten song.
Time has stolen your vibrant hue,
Leaving behind just shadows and dew.

Each gnarled twig holds a story untold,
Of summer's warmth and the winter's cold.
Yet still you reach for the azure sky,
A testament of endurance that will not die.

The whispers of seasons, now soft and slow,
Carried by breezes through valleys below.
With every sigh, your stories release,
An elegy woven in silence and peace.

Beneath the earth, roots stretch and weave,
A network of secrets the trees believe.
Though branches may wither, and leaves may fall,
Life blooms anew in the heart of it all.

So stand tall, dear branches, though time may forsake,
You cradle the past in your gentle ache.
In every scar, there's a tale that remains,
Of sorrows and joys, of losses and gains.

Tales from the Gnarled Roots

Deep in the earth, where shadows intertwine,
Gnarled roots whisper, through spirits divine.
Tales of the ancients, buried and deep,
Secrets of time, in silence they keep.

With each turn of earth, with every small shift,
Stories are nestled, like a treasured gift.
The pulse of the forest, the heartbeat of time,
Resonates softly, in rhythm and rhyme.

In the warm embrace of the twilight's glow,
These roots weave together the seeds we sow.
The essence of life flows freely below,
A dance of creation, a vibrant tableau.

Fingers of ivy climb the aged bark,
Carving their pathways throughout the dark.
While shadows of history twist and twine,
In the language of nature, forever divine.

And when the night's curtain begins to fall,
The roots hold safe a silent call.
For every ending holds a story's reprise,
In the gnarled embrace, where true magic lies.

The Dance of the Hidden Sprouts

In shadows deep, where whispers play,
The hidden sprouts begin their sway.
With sunlight soft on verdant leaves,
They dance to songs that nature weaves.

A gentle breeze stirs up the ground,
As tiny roots reach out, unbound.
Each bud unfurls with hopeful grace,
A tapestry of life embraced.

The ground is rich, the air is sweet,
With every step, the moves repeat.
A glowing life beneath the stone,
In secret realms, they're not alone.

With delicate colors, they ignite,
A symphony of green delight.
In twilight's glow, they take their chance,
And sway as if in timeless dance.

Awake, arise, the world anew,
In every drop of morning dew.
The dance begins, the time is now,
With nature's strength behind the bow.

Enchanted Silence of the Woodlands

In the heart where shadows lie,
The woodlands breathe, a gentle sigh.
Between the trees, the whispers flow,
In secrets held, the wonders grow.

Each rustling leaf, a voice in tune,
A melody beneath the moon.
The silence weaves a sacred spell,
Where ancient stories live and dwell.

Mossy carpets, soft and deep,
Where woodland creatures come to sleep.
In hidden nooks, a life unfolds,
With every tale, a thousand golds.

The brook it hums, the owls it calls,
As twilight drapes its velvet shawls.
Magic lingers in the air,
Enchanted solace everywhere.

So wander deep, let your heart roam,
In silence find your spirit's home.
For in the woodlands, echo true,
A world of dreams awaits for you.

Portrait of a Timeworn Forest

Each gnarled tree, a tale to tell,
Of ages passed and magic's spell.
In scarred bark and branches bare,
The whisper of a timeless flare.

Moss drapes softly, nature's veil,
A painted canvas, rich and pale.
With every twist and winding root,
A portrait forged, in silence, mute.

Beneath the canopy, shadows play,
In hues of green and shades of gray.
The forest breathes with wisdom old,
In every creak, its secrets told.

A symphony of life rings clear,
As creatures scurry, drawing near.
From golden sun to silver night,
A world exists beyond our sight.

And so we stand, in awe, amazed,
By every leaf and sun-drenched haze.
A timeworn forest, strong and true,
In every glance, a life anew.

Cradle of Life in Decay

Amidst the fallen leaves and dust,
Lies beauty wrapped in nature's trust.
In quiet corners, life abides,
A cradle where the circle rides.

Decay may seem a fearsome plight,
Yet from its cloak, new dreams take flight.
Each crumb of earth, a seed reborn,
In darkness deep, the light is sworn.

With every rusted, twisted root,
A promise lingers, in pursuit.
Through bramble thick, and shadows cast,
A new beginning blooms at last.

So dance the dance of life once more,
Where every end is but a door.
Embrace the cycle, soft and slow,
In decay's arms, new wonders grow.

This cradle holds the wildest dreams,
In nature's hands, the world redeems.
Through death, we find what lives anew,
In every breath, the cycle's true.

Footprints in the Velvet Moss

Beneath the boughs the shadows play,
Tiny prints mark the soft, green sway.
Nature whispers secrets, soft and low,
In the heart of the forest where wild things grow.

A dance of light through leaves does weave,
Each step a promise, make you believe.
Footfalls echo where wildflowers bloom,
In the twilight's embrace, dispelling the gloom.

The velvet moss cradles wonders rare,
A tapestry woven with delicate care.
Yet, each footfall is fleeting and light,
Leaving traces just lost to the night.

As time flows onward, it gently erases,
The stories told in the forest's embraces.
Yet in our hearts, those spells remain,
Footprints in moss, a sweet, soft refrain.

Murmurs of the Receding Light

As dusk settles over the quiet glen,
Murmurs are heard, soft as a pen.
The sun bids farewell, with hues of gold,
Whispering secrets the night will hold.

Stars awaken in the velvet sky,
Winking softly, a brotherly sigh.
The moon casts shadows on paths below,
In the gathering dark, where dreams start to flow.

Listen closely to the night's lullaby,
Faint echoes of laughter, a distance sigh.
The world slows down, as the twilight glows,
In this serene calm, pure magic bestows.

The breeze carries tales, of long-ago fights,
Return with the dawn, love's pure delights.
Yet now we cherish the secrets so bright,
In murmurs of dusk, the world feels right.

Ode to the Decaying Petals

Once vibrant blooms that danced in the sun,
Now look how gracefully their colors run.
Petals like whispers drift gently to ground,
In their gentle fading, beauty is found.

A tapestry woven with hints of the past,
Each petal a story, both fragile and vast.
Time's patient caress, the art of decay,
Breathes life into memories that fade away.

Their fragrance lingers, though they wither and fall,
An ode to the moments, we cherish them all.
In gardens of time, where colors once reigned,
In each solemn fall, a remembrance is gained.

For in every ending, a new start awaits,
The cycle of life, where love never hesitates.
So here in the twilight, we honor the frail,
The decaying petals, their stories regale.

Treasures Among the Unkempt

Amidst the wild, where chaos takes hold,
Lie hidden treasures, waiting to unfold.
Unkempt gardens with stories untold,
Whisper of magic, a dance of the bold.

Rusted keys and trinkets of gold,
Echoes of laughter, tales to behold.
Nature's embrace, wild and free,
Nurturing secrets of what used to be.

Wildflowers bloom in defiance of care,
Each petal a canvas, in vivid flair.
Within the disorder, life finds a way,
To blossom in moments where wild hearts play.

Forgotten paths where the brave would dream,
Reveal the magic in nature's gleam.
Treasures await in the untamed wild,
As we wander through worlds, forever beguiled.

The Solace of Withered Petals

In twilight's hush, the petals sigh,
Their colors fade, as dreams pass by.
Among the shadows, whispers linger,
Of love once held by gentle fingers.

As autumn's breath claims amber leaves,
A tale unfolds, as heart believes.
The crumpled blooms hold secrets tight,
Of fleeting time and lost delight.

In gardens where the shadows wane,
Withered petals nurse the pain.
Yet in their frailty, hope abides,
For beauty lingers where love resides.

Beneath the stars, they tell their lore,
Of dreams that danced and hearts that soar.
In silence wrapped, their echoes play,
A memory that won't decay.

Reveries of the Woodland Temple

In forest deep, where whispers dwell,
A temple stands, with magic well.
Its ancient stones, they breathe of lore,
Of woodlands rich and hearts that soar.

With mossy arches, time does weave,
A tapestry of hope to grieve.
Each sunbeam filtered through the leaves,
Unfolds tales that the forest weaves.

In unity, the shadows blend,
As nature sings, they will not end.
The souls who wander, quick and slow,
Find peace within the boughs that grow.

With every breeze, a whisper calls,
Through soaring pines and ivy walls.
In twilight's grace, the spirits dance,
Inviting hearts to take a chance.

Chronicles of the Gnarled Sentinel

Beneath the sky, the gnarled old tree,
With twisted limbs, so wild and free.
Its bark is etched with tales untold,
Of lovers lost and dreams of gold.

In summer's glow and winter's chill,
It stands a guard; silent, still.
A hundred seasons it has braved,
Through storms and calm, its form is graved.

The winds do whisper secrets near,
Of those who ventured, hearts sincere.
With every sigh, it charts the past,
A witness to the die is cast.

A timeworn sage with knowing eyes,
It hears the songs of sorrowed sighs.
In muted shadows, dreams take flight,
The gnarled sentinel stands in light.

Beneath the Embrace of Elder Trees

In woods where whispers weave and wind,
The elder trees with stories pinned.
Their branches cradle secrets rare,
In twilight's hush, a world laid bare.

With roots entwined in soil so deep,
They guard the secrets that we keep.
Each creak and groan, a whispered plea,
In harmony, they cradle me.

The dances of the fireflies glint,
Illuminate where shadows hint.
While starlight weaves through twilight's song,
In nature's heart, we all belong.

Beneath their watch, I find my place,
In stillness wrapped, I feel their grace.
As nature hums its ancient tune,
The elder trees, beneath the moon.

The Hidden World of the Shade

In twilight's hush, where secrets grow,
Beneath the trees, where soft winds blow.
A realm of whispers, shadows gleam,
In every corner, magic's dream.

The creek that murmurs, tales of old,
Painted with starlight, wrapped in gold.
Among the ferns, the fae do dance,
In nature's waltz, they take their chance.

A flicker, a shimmer, in the night,
Glimmers of wonder, pure delight.
In every nook, where hush prevails,
The shade conceals, as night unveils.

With every step, the path is spun,
Into the world where dreams can run.
And if you listen, deep and clear,
The Shade will share what you may hear.

So tread with care, and hold your breath,
Embrace the silence, dance with death.
For in this hidden, shadowed land,
The beauty lies, will you understand?

A Commune of Shadow and Silence

In shadows deep, where whispers cling,
A world unfolds, an unseen spring.
The moon a guardian, soft and bright,
Guiding lost souls through the night.

Among the willows, silence sings,
A captive tune, of delicate things.
In every sigh, the echoes blend,
A commune found, in twilight's end.

Beneath the stars, the owls take flight,
Weaving shadows with threads of light.
A tapestry rare, where moments weave,
In quiet partnership, we believe.

The cool breeze carries a tale so grand,
Of ancient bonds, and whispered strands.
In harmony's heart, we find our place,
In shadow's embrace, we leave a trace.

So linger long, let silence speak,
In the commune of peace, we all seek.
Where shadows dance, and secrets thrive,
In this sacred space, we come alive.

The Brew of Nature's Alchemy

In cauldrons deep, where potions brew,
Nature whispers, old yet new.
A pinch of starlight, a dash of rain,
Mix with shadows, reduce the pain.

The leaves confide in gentle tones,
Each herb a story, replete with bones.
As wildflowers bloom in radiant sprawl,
The alchemists hear the forest's call.

With bark and berry, root and seed,
The potion simmers, fulfilling need.
In every swirl, in colors bright,
The magic waits to share its light.

Through thickets dense, the echoes rise,
In nature's forge, no need for lies.
When tinctures made bring peace anew,
Nature's alchemy, pure and true.

So gather 'round, both young and old,
For wisdom lies in secrets told.
In every sip, a tale of grace,
The brew of life, in nature's embrace.

Whispers of Painted Leaves

In autumn's grasp, the leaves confide,
With colors bold, they dance and slide.
Each whisper carries a tale untold,
A legacy woven in red and gold.

The breeze composes a gentle song,
As branches sway, where shadows throng.
With every rustle, a secret sigh,
In painted leaves, the past comes by.

Amber and auburn, a vibrant blend,
The trees hold stories, without an end.
In twilight's glow, let silence weave,
The magic found in autumn's leave.

As twilight dances on edges sharp,
The world transforms, a vibrant arc.
With hushed tones, the leaves engage,
In quiet corners, they turn the page.

So let us gather these whispers dear,
In every flutter, cast aside fear.
For in the rustle, wisdom thrives,
In painted leaves, the heart derives.

The Tempest of Tender Roots

In shadows deep, where whispers play,
The tender roots find their own way.
They stretch and reach, though skies may roar,
In silent strength, they yearn for more.

The tempest howls, a mighty breath,
Yet life persists beyond such strife.
With every gust, they weave their fate,
Resilient hearts that never wait.

Beneath the storm, the earth does sigh,
As tendrils grasp and stones defy.
With every pulse, they push and pry,
To seek the sun, they climb and try.

Though chaos reigns, they hold their ground,
In muddy depths, new dreams are found.
The tempest's wrath brings forth the bloom,
In darkest nights, sweet scents consume.

For every trial that roots endure,
A stronger bond, a love that's pure.
Through roughest seas, they still will rise,
To touch the stars and kiss the skies.

Signals from the Understory

Beneath the boughs, where whispers dwell,
The secrets of the forest swell.
With every leaf, a tale is spun,
Of battles fought and races run.

In shaded glades, the stories bloom,
From tiny ferns to flowers' plume.
Each pulse of life, a gentle breath,
A symphony of love and death.

The danced choreography of light,
Unfolds on leaves, both day and night.
The earth replies with tiny signs,
Connections made through verdant vines.

From roots entwined, a message sent,
The stories join, though time is spent.
In silence deep, the truth reveals,
The strength of life, the love it feels.

So heed the signals from below,
In every shadow, life will grow.
For in the dark, the dreams ignite,
And weave the fabric of their flight.

The Lullaby of the Unseen

In whispering woods, where shadows play,
The unseen sings at close of day.
With gentle hum and softest cheer,
They weave a world for hearts to hear.

The nightingale, a lullaby sweet,
Calls forth the stars from their retreat.
In every breath, a secret shared,
A melody where none have dared.

The unseen tenders, a silent grace,
Caress the dreams in their embrace.
With silver threads of moonlit glow,
They whisper truths that few will know.

As leaves do dance to nature's tune,
The spirits stir beneath the moon.
In slumber deep, they guard the night,
And cradle hopes until the light.

So close your eyes and feel their song,
The unseen waits where you belong.
In harmony, the world will spin,
And in the silence, let love begin.

Songs of the Lowly Saplings

In humble plots where lowly stand,
The saplings stretch, reach for the land.
With fragile limbs and soft green hue,
They dream of skies, of rain, and dew.

Each gentle breeze sings them to grow,
With whispered secrets that only they know.
Through trials hard, they seek the sun,
A journey started, never undone.

In tender roots, their hopes reside,
And through the storms, they still abide.
Their laughter dances on the air,
As they embrace what's light and fair.

The songs they sing are pure and sweet,
A chorus bright where earth and sky meet.
For in each leaf, a story told,
Of visions bright and hearts so bold.

So gather near and lend an ear,
To songs of saplings, calm and clear.
For in their strength, a lesson shines,
That life, though small, in time aligns.

Whispers Beneath the Ancient Boughs

In the twilight hush, where shadows lie,
Whispers dance soft like a lullaby.
Ancient boughs sway with secrets deep,
Guardians of dreams where the lost souls weep.

Moss-covered stones, all worn and gray,
Hear the tales of the passing day.
Creatures of night begin to stir,
Caressing the air with a gentle whir.

Moonbeams weave through leaves and light,
Casting magic in the thickening night.
A chorus of crickets plays its tune,
Beneath the watchful gaze of the moon.

Each rustle tells of the time that's flown,
Of battles fought, and love that's grown.
In whispers soft, the woodlands sigh,
A tapestry woven in every sigh.

Among the roots where the fairies dwell,
Lies the history only trees can tell.
With every breath of the midnight air,
The ancient boughs hold a timeless prayer.

Shadows of the Forgotten Grove

Amidst the ruins, where silence speaks,
The forgotten grove hides within its peaks.
Shadows twist in a delicate dance,
Luring the souls lost in a trance.

In the dusk's embrace, the branches weave,
Stories of joy, of love, and leave.
Each leaf a memory, each breeze a song,
Echoing softly where they belong.

Footfalls echo on the dampened ground,
Whispers of wanderers forever crowned.
Specters drift through the misty haze,
Writing the past with their ancient ways.

Glimmers of light through the darkened wood,
Effecting changes as only it could.
In shadows deep, the magic thrives,
Where time is still and the heart survives.

The grove holds tales like the stars in the sky,
Secrets entwined in a soft lullaby.
With every heartbeat, the stories grow,
In silence profound, the shadows flow.

Echoes in the Twilight Thicket

In the twilight thicket, where echoes play,
Dreams take flight as night turns to day.
Moonlit whispers float through the leaves,
Telling tales of what one believes.

Starlit paths weave through branches bare,
Secrets shared in the cool night air.
Rustling leaves join the evening song,
Calling out to those who've wandered long.

Dew-kissed petals glimmer with cheer,
Nature's embrace draws all those near.
The midnight owl hoots a soft refrain,
Guiding the lost through passion and pain.

With every rustle comes the winds' caress,
Promises whispered in gentle finesse.
In the thicket's heart, where stories blend,
Hope and wonder shall never end.

Each echo a memory that time can't erase,
Carved in the shadows, the night's warm embrace.
Beneath the stars, beneath the bough,
Life's fleeting moments, the here and now.

Secrets of the Timid Saplings

Amongst the twilight, small saplings sway,
Harboring secrets of a world at play.
Their timid forms stretch towards the light,
Yearning for dreams that take flight at night.

With each gentle breeze, they flutter and twist,
Sharing soft whispers of paths not missed.
Roots digging deep in the cool, rich earth,
Nurturing hopes, igniting their birth.

In the hush of dusk, their shadows grow,
Dancing and twirling in a twilight glow.
Every heartbeat in their tender frame,
Keeps the nature of life, quiet yet untame.

As stars begin to twinkle above,
The saplings dream of the life they'll love.
Secrets of seasons in every shade,
Woven with care, their glories portrayed.

In this enchanted hour, where whispers convene,
The timid saplings unfold the unseen.
Guardians of hope, with courage so small,
Within their embrace, life dances for all.

The Lament of the Leafless Boughs

In the grip of winter's breath,
Branches stand bare, forlorn and cold,
Whispers of life now drift in death,
Memories of green, a tale retold.

Echoes of joy from seasons past,
Eager leaves danced in sunlit cheer,
Yet time's cruel hand has come at last,
Silencing laughter, drawing near.

The wind carries secrets long forgot,
Boughs creak and sway, a mournful tune,
Nature's symphony of what is not,
Under the watch of a waning moon.

Yet beneath the frost, a promise lies,
Slumbering hopes in the chill of night,
Awakening dreams as the sunlight sighs,
Leafless boughs yearn for the dawn's delight.

And when spring brushes life anew,
The boughs, once barren, will bloom once more,
In verdant hues, a vibrant view,
The leafless lament transformed to soar.

Musings on the Edge of the Wildwood

Beneath the arch of ancient trees,
Whispers echo, soft and low,
Each shadow bides a gentle breeze,
Secrets hidden where few dare go.

With every step, the world awakes,
Nature's canvas, rich and bright,
The wildwood stirs, its heartbeat quakes,
Painted in gold by waning light.

Curious creatures peek and pry,
In tangled thickets, they softly creep,
A songbird's call, a fleeting sigh,
For dreams of twilight gently seep.

The mossy ground, a welcome bed,
For weary souls seeking repose,
Here time stands still, so lightly tread,
In the hush of the wildwood's prose.

Yet not all paths are free from pain,
For shadows linger in every glade,
But beauty mingles with the mundane,
As wildwood's heart begins to fade.

Mirth of the Dappled Glade

In a sunlit nook where laughter springs,
Dancing shadows weave a story,
Each rustling leaf on whispering wings,
Bears witness to nature's pure glory.

Here, the brook hums a merry tune,
Ribbons of light through branches flow,
And daisies sway like stars by noon,
Their bloom adorned with nature's glow.

Frolicsome fawns in playful chase,
Glade rejoices, young hearts are free,
In this enchanted, sacred space,
Life unfurls like a blossoming tree.

Sunbeams sprinkle gold on this fair ground,
Joy spills forth in every breath,
Nature's spirit in laughter is found,
A boundless escape from silence and death.

So linger here, where mirth prevails,
Beneath the dappled, timeless skies,
Within this glade, all sorrow pales,
And every heart soars, ever wise.

Portents in the Stillness of the Underbrush

In the hush of night, a silence weaves,
The underbrush stirs with unseen threads,
Nature holds secrets in rustling leaves,
As twilight descends, a shiver spreads.

Beneath the surface, life seems to pause,
Yet something stirs, a pulse in the dark,
A flicker of fate, nature's own laws,
Awakens the night with a murmuring spark.

Crickets hum ancient tales of woe,
As shadows linger, waiting for light,
Each creak and crack whispers, 'Come and show,
What lies beyond this blanket of night.'

The air thrums with magic, thick and alive,
A portent of change, a promise in sight,
With each fleeting moment, visions contrive,
In stillness, the universe ignites.

So listen closely; heed the call,
For underbrush holds truths yet untold,
In stillness, the world prepares for it all,
Future unfolds, as mysteries unfold.

Echoes in the Shade of Time

In the silence where shadows play,
Whispers of yesterdays drift away.
Leaves murmur tales of long-lost dreams,
Carried by winds that weave through the seams.

Footsteps linger on paths so worn,
Ghosts of memories, softly reborn.
Beneath the boughs of the ancient oak,
Lies the truth in the words unspoke.

Time holds the echoes within its grasp,
Each secret tethered, like a gentle clasp.
Lighting the corners of twilight's embrace,
A dance of shadows in a timeless space.

In the twilight's sigh, stories entwine,
Every breath of the past, a delicate line.
The hourglass weeps with grains of gold,
As history's spine begins to unfold.

So linger awhile, in the soft twilight,
Where echoes of dreams still dance in the light.
Let the whispers cast their enchanting spell,
For within the shade, all stories dwell.

Secrets Woven in Green

In the heart of the forest, secrets lay,
Where the sun spills gold on each vibrant play.
With roots entwined in a lover's embrace,
The ancient oaks whisper of time and space.

Mossy carpets hide tales of yore,
While ferns unfold as the heartbeats soar.
Crickets hum serenades low,
In the hush of the evening, where shadows grow.

Each petal tells of a moment held tight,
In the cool, tender arms of the night.
The breeze carries songs of the earth's soft heart,
A testament to life, woven art.

Cascading waterfalls murmur and sigh,
Reflecting the dreams of the stars up high.
In this realm where the wild things play,
Secrets are born, come what may.

So wander beneath the verdant seams,
And lose yourself in the land of dreams.
For in this haven, where green is seen,
Every leaf holds a wish, pure and keen.

The Silent Watcher of the Glen

In the glen where the wild things grow,
A watcher stands still, ever so slow.
With eyes like the twilight, deep and wise,
It guards the secrets beneath the skies.

Amidst the shadows and dappled light,
It witnesses dreams that take flight.
Each breeze carries whispers, soft and mild,
As the watcher observes, both tender and wild.

Through storms that rage and sunlit days,
It sees the dance of life's complex ways.
A sentinel bound to the pulse of the earth,
Cradling the stories of death and birth.

It knows every creature, each heart that beats,
Every joy, every sorrow, that time repeats.
In the hush of dusk, when the world turns gray,
The silent watcher keeps night at bay.

So trust in the stillness, find peace in the flow,
For the watcher exists where both shadows grow.
In the secrets of nature, find solace and grace,
In the embrace of the glen, a sacred space.

Reverie of the Unseen Buds

In the cradle of dawn, when the world is still,
Unseen buds awaken with gentle thrill.
Each petal unfolding, a promise unspoken,
In the silence of morning, nature's token.

The dew-kissed whispers on vibrant green,
Reveal the dreams that have ever been.
Softly they breathe with the warmth of the sun,
Linking the past and the future as one.

In the garden of hopes, where shadows play,
These tender blooms chase the darkness away.
They weave a tapestry rich and grand,
A dance of creation through nature's hand.

Beneath the firmament, so bright and clear,
Every bud carries whispers for those who hear.
In the rush of the world, pause for a glance,
At the miracles hidden that spark and dance.

For in each tiny bud, a story lies,
Of patience and growth beneath endless skies.
So cherish the silence, the moments, the buds,
In the reverie of life where the heart truly floods.

The Mystique of Shady Realms

In twilight's hush, the shadows play,
Where whispers thread through ancient trees,
Lost secrets waltz in the fading day,
As magic drifts upon the breeze.

The moonlight spills on mossy ground,
In hidden glades, the fairies meet,
With laughter soft, they twirl around,
Their twinkling eyes in night discreet.

A brook nearby hums tales of old,
Where woodland creatures roam and hide,
In every leaf, a story told,
In every rustle, dreams abide.

Yet time, it weaves a gentle thread,
Through realms where sunlight scarce intrudes,
With shadows deep, and visions spread,
These mystic paths form secret moods.

So linger here, let thoughts unfurl,
In shady realms where wonders bloom,
Embrace the night, let spirits swirl,
And trace the stars in velvet gloom.

Where Wildflowers Once Danced

In sunlit meadows, colors bright,
Wildflowers swayed in joyful throng,
Each petal catching morning light,
They danced to nature's timeless song.

Soft breezes whispered through the field,
As bees and butterflies took flight,
In blossoms' warmth, hearts were healed,
Their fragrance lingered day and night.

But seasons changed and shadows crept,
The wildflowers bowed to the frost,
In silence, dreams and memories slept,
Of vibrant days forever lost.

Yet in the heart, their echoes stay,
Bright pigments of the past entwined,
Reminding us of life's ballet,
Where wildflowers once danced, so kind.

So cherish blooms that fade away,
For beauty lies in memory's glance,
A tapestry of yesterday,
Where wildflowers once dared to dance.

Hushed Dreams of the Overgrown

In corners where the wild things grow,
Forgotten paths weave through the green,
With secrets hushed, and tales we know,
Of whispered hopes, where dreams have been.

The ivy climbs, its fingers trace,
The stories etched on weathered stone,
In silence holds a sacred space,
For longing hearts that once roamed lone.

A crumbling wall, a child's delight,
With dappled sunbeams warming earth,
In tangled weeds, the past takes flight,
Reviving echoes of lost mirth.

In overgrown gardens, shadows blend,
With every breath, a tale reborn,
For in these dreams, we find a friend,
Amidst the weeds, hope can be worn.

So wander on, through verdant halls,
Where life is rich and hearts are free,
In hushed dreams, hear nature's calls,
In overgrown realms, find the key.

Stories of the Forgotten Flora

In quiet corners, blooms reside,
With petals soft as whispered lore,
Each flower holds a tale inside,
Of joy and sorrow, evermore.

The daisies nod, the violets sigh,
While sunlight warms the elder trees,
In gentle breezes, they comply,
To share their secrets with the leaves.

Once vibrant blooms, now shadows cast,
Reminders of the days gone by,
Their stories etched in time so vast,
Of love and loss beneath the sky.

In every stem, a journey lies,
Through seasons rich with laughter sweet,
Yet in the silence, soft replies,
Whisper of paths where fates did meet.

So pause awhile, let silence reign,
Among the flora, mysteries dwell,
In forgotten tales, joy and pain,
These stories linger, bloom as well.

www.ingramcontent.com/pod-product-compliance
Ingram Content Group UK Ltd.
Pitfield, Milton Keynes, MK11 3LW, UK
UKHW021333280125
4330UKWH00005B/508